THE GREAT WALL

长　城

FOREIGN LANGUAGES PRESS　BEIJING

外文出版社　北京

THE GREAT WALL

The Great Wall, which coils like a guardian dragon over the undulating terrain of northern China, is comparable to any other historic wonder of the world in significance and grandeur. The building and rebuilding of it reflect the ups and downs of China's dynasties over a period of more than 2,000 years.

In the days when wars were fought mainly by infantry and cavalry, sturdy city-walls and well-guarded passes were of vital importance in defence. So the Great Wall was one of the most stupendous defence works built in ancient times.

In the Spring and Autumn period (770-256 B.C.), when the various dukedoms that China was divided into were in a constant state of internecine warfare, defensive walls were built around cities and along the boundaries. After unifying all the states into the powerful Qin Dynasty in 221 B.C., Qin Shi Huang, the first emperor of the Qin Dynasty joined up the northern walls of the former states of Qin, Zhao and Yan and lengthened them to form a barrier extending more than 5,000 km. Reinforcement of the Great Wall continued throughout the following dynasties, among which the Han (206 B. C. - A. D. 220) and Ming (1368-1644) periods saw feverish efforts to shore up this huge defensive barrier. Most of the wall which can be seen today was rebuilt in the Ming Dynasty. It covers some 7,300 km, from the Shanhai Pass in Hebei Province in the east to the Jiayu Pass in Gansu Province in the west. Fortunately it retains its dignified and ancient aura as a result of good preservation.

The Great Wall has hundreds of passes and over 10,000 watchtowers. The wall, following steep terrain and displaying every variety of ancient military architecture, is the main body of what used to be China's main redoubt guarding the fertile Central Plain against the barbarian hordes. The Ming Great Wall is ten m. high and five m. wide, on average. Five horses can canter side by side along the top of it. The battlements were manned by bowmen in times of attack. The defenders were housed in forts located at strategic intervals. Also situated in a regular pattern were beacon towers which gave warning along the full length of the wall and far inland of the approach of any enemy.

There are dozens of passes on the Great Wall well-known for their magnificent views and important locations. Situated to the northeast of Qinhuangdao City in Hebei Province, the Shanhai Pass — the "No. 1 Pass On the Great Wall" — extends into the Bohai Sea at the "Old Dragon's Head," at the easternmost end of the Great Wall. The square pass joins mountainous terrain with the sea, and was easy to defend but difficult to attack. The Juyong Pass, located in a valley at Mount Yanshan, 50 km. northwest of Beijing, was built in the Ming Dynasty and is famous for the lush greenery of the hills round it. In addition, there is the delicately carved structure called Cloud Terrace at the pass. The westernmost end of the Great Wall, the Jiayu Pass, is located in Gansu Province and is preserved almost entire. It is called the "Soul of the Great Wall" for its dignified and towering structure.

As time went by, the Great Wall lost its military importance and became a historic relic much beloved of sightseers. Visitors today, standing on the top of the Great Wall, are often amazed at its awesomeness and marvel at the great power of the ancient Chinese people in conquering nature. There is an old Chinese saying that goes, "He who hasn't been to the Great Wall is not a true man," which is also a warm greeting to every tourist coming to gaze upon this wonder of the world.

The Great Wall is a milestone in the history of the world's architecture. The present well-preserved Great Wall was built in the Ming Dynasty. It extends some 6,300 km., from the Shanhai Pass in Hebei Province in the east to the Jiayu Pass in Gansu Province in the west. This album concentrates on the Great Wall skirting Beijing, and the famous scenic spots along the wall, presenting its magnificent views from different angles.

长　城

在中国广袤的土地上，从东到西横亘着一道气势宏伟的"大墙"。它跨群山、越峻岭、穿草原、过大漠，宛如一条巨龙，腾翔在中国的北方。它就是举世闻名的万里长城。长城作为世界建筑奇迹之一，已载入世界文明的史册。它的坍塌与重修，记载了中国两千年以来历代王朝的兴衰，标明历史的演进。

在主要依靠步兵和骑兵征战的时代，宽厚的城墙和坚固的关隘能够起到至关重要的防御作用。长城就是中国古代遗留下来的一种防御工程。

长城最早的筑城史，始于春秋战国时期（前 770-前 256）。彼时"王室衰微，诸侯争霸"，各诸侯国为抵御别国侵略，各自筑起漫长的城墙。此时的长城，还各自独立，互不连贯。到了秦（前 221-前 206）统一后，秦始皇将秦、赵、燕三国的北部城墙连缀起来修缮增筑，绵延 5000 多公里，建成了第一座真正意义上的长城。此后历代皆有增建，其中以汉朝（前 206-公元 220）和明朝（1368-1644）最为浩大。现今见到的多为明长城。明代长城的存留部分东自河北省山海关，西至甘肃省嘉峪关，全长 6300 多公里，因保存较为完好，可以让人们充分领略其雄伟气魄。

长城以漫长的城墙将成百座的雄关和上万座的墩台连缀一体，以其独特的建筑形式担负着昔日御敌和守望的重任。城墙，是万里长城的主体工程，墙体随山势而筑，千变万化。明长城的城墙平均高 10 米，宽约 5 米，可容五马并骑。墙上开有垛口，用于了望和射击敌人。城墙每隔一段即有一个堡垒式建筑，高的叫敌楼，用于守望和住宿；低的叫墙台，是放哨的地方。城墙上还连续设置一些独立的高台，称为烽火台。如遇敌情，就以白天燃烟，夜间放火来传递军情。关塞隘口，是平时出入长城的要道，也是重点防守的据点；城堡障堠分布在长城内外，用以驻兵防守。

万里长城上有著名关隘数十座，关关雄奇壮观，景色迥异。在河北省秦皇岛市东北，长城由燕山山脉从北向南飞身而下，直捣渤海，形成"天下第一关"山海关，入海处即是著名的长城东端点——"老龙头"。此关山海相连，关城居中，呈四方形，挟两侧的墩堡、关隘沉稳拱立，有"一夫当关，万夫莫开"的气势。俯卧于北京西北 50 多公里处的燕山峡谷之中的，是京郊著名风景胜地居庸关。此关于明代修建，由两山夹峙其间。关城内遗有雕刻精美的云台。关沟中清溪萦绕，四周层峦叠嶂，以"居庸叠翠"跻身燕京八景。明长城的最西端嘉峪关，位于甘肃省西部，是现存的长城关城中最完整的一处。关城形制宏伟，高大巍峨，坐落在一片广漠空旷的塞外天地之中，冷峻而神秘，有"长城主宰"之誉。

随着时间的推移，昔日烽烟散尽，长城已经逐渐化为一道历史的风景供后人凭吊和玩味。今日，来者更多地惊讶于它所表现出的人类改造自然的伟大力量。当我们站在长城之巅俯望山川时，它与绵绵群山与茫茫大漠一起震动我们的心魄，令人叹为观止。中国有句俗谚："不到长城非好汉。"希望世界上每一位热爱旅游的朋友都能够有机会来到中国，亲眼看一看他们心目中不可思议的奇迹——长城。

The Great Wall is a mighty defensive bulwark which has witnessed over 2,000 years of Chinese history. Its construction started in the Spring and Autumn and Warring States periods (770- 256 B.C.) and was completed in the Ming Dynasty (1368-1644). The existing Wall starts at the Jiayu Pass, Gansu Province, in the west and terminates at the Shanhai Pass, Hebei Province, in the east —'a total length of over 6,300 km.

横亘于中国北部疆域的万里长城,是古代中国遗留下来的一种军事防御工程。它的建筑历史从春秋战国(前770—前256)至明代(1368—1644)延续了2000余年。现存较为完整的明代长城西起甘肃省嘉峪关,东至河北省山海关,全长达6300多公里。

Old Dragon's Head

The eastern end of the Ming Dynasty Great Wall is actually in the sea off the coast of Hebei Province. It is called the Old Dragon's Head, as it extends to the Bohai Sea, just like the head of a huge dragon.

老龙头

是明代长城的东起点,地处河北省东部临海地区,因端头探入渤海,状如巨龙之首而得名。

Shanhai Pass ▷

The passes in the Great Wall were generally built at gaps between mountains, or at the confluences or turns of rivers and valleys. In the east of Hebei Province, jutting into the sea is the "No. 1 Pass Under Heaven," the Shanhai Pass.

山海关

长城以绵延的城墙将成百座的雄关连缀一体。关隘是防守的重点,一般设在山间峡口或河谷汇合转折之处。河北省东部临海地区的山海关,是长城东起的第一个关口,被誉为"天下第一关"。

Cloud Terrace at Juyong Pass

More than 50 km. northwest of Beijing is the Juyong Pass, one of the most famous passes in the Ming Dynasty Great Wall. In the pass there is a white marble terrace built in the Yuan Dynasty (1206-1368). The terrace bears exquisite carvings of the Four Heavenly Kings and passages from the Buddhist scriptures in six languages.

居庸关

居庸关位于北京西北 50 多公里，为明长城最负盛名的雄关之一，地势绝险、景色迷人。关城中的著名景观云台建于元代，由汉白玉砌成，上面雕有异常精美的四大天王像及六种文字撰写的经文。

Badaling Section of the Great Wall

Badaling, a famous section of the Great Wall, is located on a ridge of the Yanshan Mountains, which stand at the north end of Juyong Pass and rise to 1,000 m. above sea level. The terrain is difficult of access and a strategic position. Badaling is one of Beijing's major tourist attractions.

八达岭长城

长城著名城段,位于居庸关关沟北口,盘卧于海拔600-1000 米的燕山山脊上,是扼守京北的咽喉要道,形势十分险要。因形态完好、气魄雄浑而成为京都旅游胜地。

Badaling at sunset.
八达岭暮色。

The Great Wall after a snowfall.
雪后初霁。

The Wall at Badaling, on average 7 to 8 m. high and 6 to 7 m. wide, and with a roadway on the top 4 or 5 m. wide, was built with bricks and rectangular slabs of stone, which were carried by manpower, or such pack animals as donkeys and goats.

城墙是长城的主体,随地势而筑。以八达岭为例,墙身平均高7、8米,厚6、7米,顶宽4、5米。墙身断面呈上小下大的梯形,以整齐的条石和城砖垒砌而成,内填石块灰土,十分坚固结实。在当时,运送这些建筑材料只能靠人力、简单的机具或毛驴、山羊等畜力背运,工程极为艰巨。据载仅八达岭一段约200米的城墙,就由几千人修了半年左右的时间才完成。

Badaling is most beautiful in the fall when the leaves of the maple trees which clothe the mountains here turn an enchanting red.

金秋万山红遍,八达岭长城逶迤于一片醉人的锦绣之中。

The Wall is silent at dawn.
晨光微曦，天地悠悠。

The Great Wall in the moonlight.
晓月初升，长城与莽莽群山浑然一体，沉静而神秘。

Mutianyu Section of the Great Wall

The Mutianyu section of the Great Wall lies in Huairou County, Beijing, connecting the Ju yong Pass on the west with Gubeikou on the east. It is located in a humid zone, where plants are luxuriant and the scenery changes with the seasons. The entire section is a wonderful scenic spot along the Great Wall.

慕田峪长城

地处北京怀柔县境内,西接居庸关,东连古北口。因整段长城处于温湿地区,植被茂盛,四季景致万千,是长城沿线的一处佳景胜地。

Dajiaoloushan Section of the Great Wall ▷

The Dajiaoloushan section of the Great Wall lies southeast of Mutianyu, where three branches of the wall join together. Built with rectangular slabs of brown granite, the Wall here is very solid.

大角楼山长城

位于慕田峪东南,有三条长城盘绕汇聚于此。此处墙体由褐色花岗岩条石砌筑,十分坚固。

The Great Wall basking in golden sunshine.
秋日夕照，沐浴金辉。

◁ The Great Wall has a succession of beacon towers and watchtowers. In case of the enemy approaching, the guards on the beacon towers would send smoke signals in the daytime and light bright fires at night to convey military intelligence. The watchtowers served as accommodation for the troops and as storage places for arms.

长城上烽燧连绵,敌楼密布。烽燧即烽火台,如遇敌情,就用白天燃烟、夜间放火来传递军情;敌楼供士兵守望、住宿和储存武器之用。

The fairyland world of the Great Wall.
雾锁重楼,如抵仙境。

Gubeikou Section of the Great Wall

The Gubeikou section of the Great Wall lies in the north of Miyun County, Beijing. It was one of the strategic passages through the Yanshan Mountains.

古北口长城

位于北京密云县北部,是燕山山脉南北交通咽喉之一。主体城墙将盘龙、卧虎二山连成一线,形成奇险。图中敌楼呈罕见的圆形,据称在北京地段的长城中仅有五处。

At regular intervals along the top of the Great Wall are square breaches called crenels for keeping a lookout, beneath which are embrasures for shooting.

长城城墙的顶部，靠内侧是宇墙（或称女墙），靠外侧每隔一段有一个方形缺口，称为垛口。每个垛口上有一个小洞，用于观察敌情；垛口下的小孔叫射洞，用于射击来敌。

The Wall was originally built of loess on the plains and stone in the mountain areas. In the Ming Dynasty, however, the wall was built with bricks which had been baked in kilns set up on the spot.

修筑城墙的建筑材料往往是就地取材,在平原黄土地带取土夯筑,在崇山峻岭处取石垒砌。明朝长城开始大量采用砖砌,砖瓦都是就地开设窑厂烧制而成的。

During the Ming Dynasty the Great Wall was reinforced and extended to ward off attacks by northern nomadic tribes for more than 200 years. The Great Wall of the Ming Dynasty was built more than 600 years ago, and most of it still towers over valleys and summits of mountains.

明王朝为抵御北方的游牧民族,在其统治的 200 多年中一直持续修筑长城,最终将其完善为一套严密的军事防御体系。明代修建的长城距今已有 600 余年历史,经历数世纪风雨,大部分仍屹立于山巅、峡谷之中。

Jinshanling Section of the Great Wall

The Jinshanling section of the Great Wall lies in the Yanshan Mountains, where Luanping County, Hebei Province, and Miyun County, Beijing, meet. It is more than 20 km. long, with over 100 watchtowers, which are much more thickly dotted than those on other sections of the Great Wall.

金山岭长城

地处河北省滦平县与北京密云县交界地区的燕山山脉,因修建在大小金山上而得名。全长 20 余公里,有敌楼 100 多座,其密集程度为长城其他地段所罕见。

Winding over a vast snowfield.
莽莽雪原，山舞银蛇。

The mist gives the Great Wall an eerie look. ▷
腾云驾雾。

Snaking endlessly across the mountains.
纵横驰骋，千山飞度。

Under a clear sky after rain.
雨后初晴。

At tranquil dusk.
风烟俱静，天山共色。

A magnificent, miraculous fairyland.
雄关夕照,残阳如血,呈现出一片金碧辉煌的神奇幻境。

The old Great Wall has many a story to tell.
古老的城垣，历经风云变幻，述说着无言的历史。

Simatai Section of the Great Wall
The Simatai section of the Great Wall lies in the northeast of Miyun County, Beijing. The Tower for Viewing the Capital (*above*).

司马台长城
纵伸于北京密云县东北,建在燕山峰巅之上,地势险峻,建筑形式奇特多样,被誉为"长城之最"。上图为司马台长城的制高点——望京楼,海拔 986 米。

The Fairy's Tower.
仙女楼昂然而立，俯瞰群山。

"Hawks Flying on Their Backs"
This section of the Great Wall lies in Huairou County, Beijing. It has the name because the peaks here look like hawks' open beaks.

鹰飞倒仰
在怀柔县境内,是西线长城与北线长城的汇合点。此处山峰状如鹰嘴,仰向青天,城墙绵延于刀削似的峰脊之上,故称"鹰飞倒仰"。

**Jiankou Section
of the Great Wall**
The Jiankou section of the
Great Wall, some 10 km.
southwest of the Mutianyu section, is located on steep cliffs,
forming a formidable natural
barrier.

箭扣长城
位于慕田峪长城西南10多公里
处，城墙修筑在数十丈深的悬岩
绝壁之上，拥有"擦边过"、"翻身
下海"、"石门"等天险。

Boundless mountains and impregnable passes.
危岭雄关，屹立千秋。

Dazhenyu Section of the Great Wall
The Dazhenyu section of the Great Wall lies in Huairou County, Beijing. The mountain slopes here are gorgeous in the fall, when the maple leaves turn red.

大榛峪长城
位于北京怀柔县境内，距北京市区约 80 公里。此处景色优美，每逢秋季，霜叶似火。

Magnificent scenery accompanies the Great Wall along its whole length. ▷
北国江山，秋意盎然。

In summer the grass, bushes and trees are verdant and luxuriant.

夏日到来，草木葱茏。

The lookout crenels here follow the line of an unbroken clifftop.

此处山势陡直而下，城段因地制宜，将垛口建为锯齿状。

"Ox-Horn Wall"

The "Ox-Horn Wall" located on a mountain ridge 940
m. above sea level northwest of the Mutianyu section
of the Great Wall. It is so called because it runs in the
shape of an ox-horn.

牛犄角边长城

高踞于慕田峪长城西北海拔 940 米高的山脊上,其势若劲
牛之牴,苍雄浑阔。

Tiekuangyu

Tiekuangyu lies in Huairou County, Beijing, 80 km. from the city proper of Beijing. It connects Huanghuacheng in the west with Dazhenyu in the east.

铁矿峪

位于北京怀柔县洞台乡,距北京80公里,西接黄花城,东连大榛峪。

Huanghuacheng Pass

The Huanghuacheng Pass, about 35 km. northwest of Huairou, Beijing, guards the northern approach to Beijing.

黄花城关

位于北京怀柔县西北约 35 公里处,把守着北京的北大门,东有古北口,西有居庸关,战略地位十分重要。

Adjacent to the Great Wall is the ▷ Huanghuacheng Reservoir, both ends of whose dams connect with the Great Wall. In the rainy season water cascades over the dam, forming a waterfall, over which a rainbow appears when the sun shines.

此城段因毗邻黄花城水库而闻名。水库大坝的两端与长城相连接,雄伟壮观。雨季,湖水从坝顶飞流而下形成瀑布,映出彩虹。

Zhuangdaokou Pass

The Zhuangdaokou Pass, in the northwest of Huairou County, Beijing, was built in the Ming Dynasty.

撞道口关

古称镇虏关,位于怀柔县西北,东临磨石口,南近黄花城。关城建于明代,是当时的一处重要隘口。

Xishuiyu Section of the Great Wall
The Xishuiyu section of the Great Wall, 30 km. southwest of Huairou County, Beijing, connects the Huanghuacheng and Longquanyu sections of the Great Wall.

西水峪长城
位于北京怀柔县西南 30 公里处，东连黄花城，西接龙泉峪。

Jiumenkou Section of the Great Wall
The Jiumenkou section of the Great Wall lies at the junction of Hebei and Liaoning provinces, 15 km. northeast of Shanhai Pass. Jiumenkou section of the Great Wall was built across the Jiujiang River, the only section of the wall spanning a body of water.

九门口长城
位于辽宁省与河北省的交界处,位于山海关长城东北15公里处。此
段长城利用峡谷的九江河天堑,跨河而建,修筑了边河城桥、围城和
城墙,形成了独特的长城险隘。

Wuqiaoling Section of the Great Wall

The Wuqiaoling section of the Great Wall lies in the Tianzhu Tibetan Autonomous County. Since it is arid here, the Wall was built by tamping local loess clay. The remains of the Wall are about 3-4 m. high.

乌鞘岭长城

位于甘肃省天祝藏族自治县境内,因地处干旱地区,城墙由黄土夯筑,现存高度约为3～4米。

Jiayu Pass

The Jiayu Pass, west of the city of Jiayuguan, Gansu Province, is the western end of the Ming Dynasty Great Wall. The Wall 7.5 km. north of the Jiayu Pass where it climbs a steep precipice (*above*).

嘉峪关

位于甘肃省嘉峪关市西，是明代长城的西止之处。经修复是现今最大最完整的一座关城。上图为悬壁长城的一段，位于嘉峪关北7.5公里的黑山坡上。因城段攀建于高150米、呈45度倾斜的山脊上而得名。

Yangguan Pass Ruins

The Yangguan Pass, 70 km. southwest of Dunhuang, Gansu Province, was a strategic gateway on the "Silk Road" and an important trade route from ancient China to west Asia.

阳关遗址

在甘肃省敦煌市西南 70 公里,自古是"丝绸之路"上的重要关隘,因位于玉门关之南而称阳关。此处因地连漠北,荒无人烟,古人咏有"劝君更进一杯酒,西出阳关无故人"的诗句。

Yumen Pass Ruins

The Yumen Pass built in the Han Dynasty (206 B.C.-A.D. 220), was located in the desert 80 km. northwest of Dunhuang, Gansu Province. The beacon towers here were built with local sandstone, reeds and tamarisks.

玉门关遗址

位于甘肃敦煌西北80公里处的戈壁滩,为汉代所建,是当时中原通往西域的重要门户。相传由西域进贡的美玉,皆取道此关进入,玉门关因之得名。其烽燧由砂石、芦苇和红柳枝搭建而成。

The Great Wall is the pride of the Chinese nation.
长城已铸成一段历史,演绎着中华民族的自豪与骄傲。

位 置 图
Wall of China

金山岭
Jinshanling

辽宁省
Liaoning Province

八达岭
Badaling

沈阳
Shenyang

内蒙古自治区
r Mongolia Autonomous Region

北京
Beijing

居庸关
Juyong Pass

山海关
Shanhai Pass

山西省
Shanxi Province

天津
Tianjin

太原
Taiyuan

河北省
Hebei Province

银川
Yinchuan

宁夏回族自治区
Ningxia Hui Autonomous Region

西安
Xi'an

慕田峪
Mutianyu

老龙头
Old Dragon's Head

甘肃省
Gansu Province

陕西省
Shaanxi Province

图书在版编目(CIP)数据

长城/兰佩瑾、曹蕾编;翟东风摄影。—北京:外文出版社,1997.5
ISBN 7-119-02055-2

Ⅰ.长… Ⅱ.①兰… ②曹… ③翟… Ⅲ.长城-摄影集 Ⅳ.K928.71-64
中国版本图书馆 CIP 数据核字(97)第 03107 号

Edited by: Lan Peijin   Cao Lei
Photos by: Zhai Dongfeng
Text by: Cao Lei
Designed by: Yuan Qing

编辑: 兰佩瑾   曹 蕾
摄影: 翟东风
撰文: 曹 蕾
设计: 元 青

长 城

兰佩瑾 曹 蕾 编 翟东风 摄影

The Great Wall

ISBN 7-119-02055-2

ⓒ Foreign Languages Press
Published by Foreign Languages Press
24 Baiwanzhuang Road,Beijing 100037,China
Printed in the People's Republic of China

ⓒ 外文出版社
外文出版社出版
(中国北京百万庄大街 24 号)
邮政编码 100037
深圳当纳利旭日印刷有限公司印刷
1997 年(24 开)第一版
1997 年第一版第一次印刷
(英汉)
ISBN 7-119-02055-2/J・1404(外)
003900 (精)